CROCHET

FOR BEGINNERS BIBLE

From Beginners to Masters in less than 5 days with this crash course and step-by-step pictures

WRITTEN BY:

PAIGE FRENCH

Table of Contents

Introduction

Crocheting is a fun activity for most ages. Crocheting can be done by children, teenagers, adults, and seniors. It is a great hobby to have because it is relaxing and enjoyable.

The craft was originally invented in Tibet as a way to keep warm. This was discovered by a Chinese man who saw the Tibetan people wearing sweaters made out of wool and decided to create his own crochet sweaters.

Crochet is a type of needlework in which yarn is made into a fabric using a hooked needle. The name is derived from the French term "crocheteur," which means "one who crochets." Crochet is a form of needlework that involves creating elongated stitches made by passing a hook through the loops of yarn, thread, or other materials to create a variety of textured fabrics. It is one of the oldest forms of textile production.

Crochet is a great hobby that can be very relaxing. There are many beautiful and practical things you can make with crochet, like blankets, hats, scarves, and even clothing. Crochet is a craft that is easy to learn for beginners, but there are some things you need to know before you start. This book will explain the basics and show you how to get started with crochet.

Crochet is one of those crafts that can seem a little intimidating at first, but with the right tools and some practice, it can be a fun craft for all ages.

Crochet is an ancient craft that has been around for centuries. It's a great skill to learn, and it's also very relaxing. Crochet is a fun, easy way to get into the craft world. It's also a great way to get into knitting, but it's easier.

Learning how to crochet is a wonderful hobby for anyone of any age. Crochet is the art of creating fabric with a hook or needles. It's different from knitting since it uses a single thread rather than two or more. There are tons of benefits to learning crochet, and it's a great skill for beginners. From making blankets, hats to home decor, you can do so much with a simple crochet hook. It also helps you build hand-eye coordination and dexterity.

Crochet is one of the oldest fiber arts as it has been around for hundreds of years. Crochet is a form of needlework that has been around for centuries and is still popular today. It doesn't take much money to get started and most beginner crochet projects are small, they make for great gifts.

Crochet is a very popular hobby for many people, and it's easy to understand why. Crochet can be incredibly relaxing and calming. It's also a great way to make beautiful creations for your home. Crochet is a great hobby for beginners because it's relatively easy to learn, requires little in the way of materials, and you can use all sorts of different stitches to create your own projects (or follow patterns others have made).

Crochet for beginners is really easy. You don't need to know how to make patterns or stitches, you just need to know the basic crochet stitches and some skills like starting chains, slip stitch, and increasing and decreasing. Crochet is a versatile art form that allows you to make both practical and decorative items. Crochet is a great craft for beginners. It's easy to learn, and the basic stitches are all very similar and easy to master. Crochet is also very portable, as you can crochet anywhere, anytime—particularly on public transportation!

Chapter 1:
History of Crochet

We do not know many things regarding the early origins of crochet because the ancient textiles that survived are very few. Some claim that originally, women used fingers to create loops and chains.

Only later did they begin to use a tool very similar to the current hook which was initially made of wood, bone, or bamboo and then in ivory and amber.

The oldest form, considered a precursor of crochet, comes from Jutland. It is a woolen cap that dates to about 3100 years ago. However, primitive textile samples were found in every corner of the globe—Far East, Asia, North and South America, and Europe.

Some scholars believe that Tambour's work was at the origin of modern crochet. This technique was used in China. It required the use of a fine hook to weave threads through a netted background.

This technique arrived in France around 1720.

An American scholar, Mary Thomas, believes that crochet work originally comes from the Arabian Peninsula. From there it spread eastward, in Tibet, and to the west, in Spain and then, thanks to merchants and sailors, even in other parts of the world.

The most delicate crochet form originated in Italy in the 16th century and was used by the sisters for making ornaments and vestments. It was considered a typical occupation within the monasteries where sisters created precious laces using very thin yarns. The linen for the altars was fitted with crocheted borders, not only for decorative purposes but also to make it more durable. Very soon, it spread to Spain and Ireland, which were very Catholic countries.

Only in the 19th century did crochet begin to be appreciated by the bourgeoisie and the nobles. The laces were used to adorn the linen of the house and underwear. Laces, finished with precious scallops full of picots and various decorations, had a huge development, especially among the ladies of the bourgeoisie, and they adorned their precious clothes with collars, gaskets, and tippets.

The crochet, which until then was not considered a genre, developed to mimic the difficult points of Venetian lace. The work was faster than needle and bobbin lace and tools were simpler and easier to find.

Perhaps its popularity took off from a lady of French origin, Eleonore Rego de la Branchiomere, who settled in Ireland, where she remained impressed by the delicacy of the work of the nuns in a convent in Dublin. She not only perfected their skills but spoke of the art of crochet in her magazine "The Needle." She also published eleven books, which contained conversion tables from needle lace and bobbin lace to crochet.

She is commonly credited with the invention of the Irish Lace. When times were hard, women had to find ways of supporting their families. This was particularly true during and after the great potato famine of the 1840s when crochet became the sole economic support. Another factor that contributed to the spread of crochet was the creation of a kind of domestic industry born in Clones to help the poorest families, thanks to Cassandra Hand, the wife of a local parish priest. The clone lace, still widely known, is a variant of Venetian lace. The Venetian lace, although very beautiful, required considerable time and Irish women found that by using the crochet hook, they could achieve the same effect in less time. These women reproduced elements linked to their environment—shamrocks, fern, brambles, wild roses, daisies, or star-shaped figures.

When Queen Victoria promoted the crochet lace in an exhibition of arts in London, fashion took off. Soon, demand became so high that professional sellers took the place of charities and the activity of lace turned from survival activities into an industry. The patterns of crocheted lace began to be written and distributed. Irish girls traveled to other parts of the world to teach crocheted lace.

From the Irish lace came the Orvieto lace, which, over the years, has acquired a peculiarity and original identity. In 1907, the Ars Wattana, a "patronage for young workers" was born. It sought to carry out the activity of production and packaging of lace and frill with special ornamental details for the Duomo of Orvieto, aimed at strengthening and developing local crafts.

The popularity of crochet reached its peak between 1910 and 1920, with the fashion of the Edwardian era. Its models were more complex stitches and the prevalence of white yarn. They began to be printed in series of books with crochet patterns that took the place of honor in the decoration and creation of clothes and household items.

In 1930, fashion acquired simpler features. Art Deco was the trend of the moment, and crochet was used primarily for garments of children and infants, christening gowns, gloves, and blankets. During the Second world war, yarn was rationed and since crocheting wastes more yarn than knitting, crochet seemed to be doomed.

Even though crochet was all the rage in Europe, it had not really gained much popularity in America. Most women who crocheted were immigrants who loved the availability of ready-made threads and other materials.

After the turn of the century, America finally accepted crochet and it became part of the many skills taught to young girls. It was considered a leisure activity since it did not produce a functional or marketable good. It was pretty much reserved for the middle and upper classes.

In the 60oths crochet came back strongly in vogue after a long hibernation, using the vivid colors of granny squares.

Crochet's popularity continued to grow until the 70oths, with ponchos being the must-have accessories.

In the 80oths, crochet began to fall out of favor. The economy was growing, and more women were working, thus having less time for crafts. Plus, crochet work was no longer affordable.

Crochet and knitting lost their importance even in the school curriculum— nobody taught it anymore, and the new generation had no time to learn. This time, it seemed that crochet was really facing extinction.

Fortunately, since the middle of the 90ths, crochet has experienced a new period of interest. Crochet can be seen today as a hobby, but for those who have awareness, they consider it an art form.

Chapter 2:
Types of Crochet

Amigurumi Crochet

This type of crochet is said to have originated from Japan. People would use this type of crochet when making toys that would be stuffed using this crochet. Ami means knitting or yarn that has been crocheted, while amigurumi means a doll that has been stuffed. This type of crochet is therefore useful if you want to make these stuffed dolls through the use of heavy yarn. One can also make fan items and the large novelty cushions as well as the home wears.

Aran Crochet

This is a type of crochet that is normally ribbed and also one that is intertwined. It is a traditional type of crochet made through interlocking threads or twines and yarns. Through this type of crocheting, you can make sweaters and chunky beanies as well as scarves. This type of crocheting is said to produce very strong items as a result of the interlocking of the cables. This is the reason why people use it to make items that would need to be worn for longer periods. They can also be used to make blankets and aphgans as well as jackets and coats and also scarves.

Bavarian Crochet

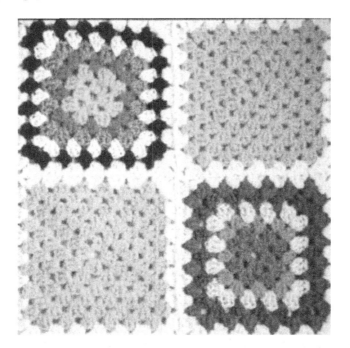

This is a type of crochet that is said to work just like the granny squares, which were traditionally made. It is used when one wants to make very thick items and also to blend in different colors when making them. This type of crochet is said to allow people to be able to blend in different colors without experiencing any challenges. They can do this by working on each part on its own. This helps them be able to blend them together, which makes them come up with a very fancy item. The granny squares make it very appealing since one can even use squares of different colors. You can make blankets and shawls through the use of Bavarian crochet.

Bosnian Crochet

Bosnian crochet is used when one wants to make dense and knit-like materials through the use of a crochet slip sew-up. You have to, however, stitch different parts of a stitch on the current row to ensure that the stitches are different in each row. You can achieve this through the use of the Bosnian crochet hooks, which are said to produce very good crochets. You can still work with the normal hooks; even the Bosnian hooks give better crochets than the other hooks.

This type of crochet is not very popular. This is because one would think that it is normal knitting when you look at the crochet. It is easy to work with it since the style used is easy to learn. People use it when they are scarves and beanies, as well as when crocheting items that do not require much time to be crocheted.

Bullion Crochet

This is a type of crochet that requires one to use a lot of time. One uses many wraps of the yarn, which have to be put around a very long hook. By doing this, you come up with a very unique stitch. This type of crochet is used when one needs to make the motifs and not when making crochets that require one to use the fabrics.

It takes a lot of time to produce the item if you are making using this type of crochet since one has to be very keen when coming up with the patterns. The final product is normally very firm and thick, as well as stiff. A crocheter uses a method to make items that are meant to be long-lasting. You can make mats out of stiff materials when they use this type of crocheting. This can help you be able to come up with very unique and firm products, so they can be used for a very long time without them wearing out.

Broomstick Crochet

This type of crochet is also called jiffy lace. It is normally made through the use of traditional crochet hooks. One form makes some stitches all around a very long as well as a wide stick that looks like that one of a broomstick. In this modern age, people are said to use large crochet hooks as well as the thick dowel when they are making the broomstick lace nowadays. It is a skill that people need to take their time to learn for them to come up with a well-made crochet. It is, however, a type of crochet that is said to produce crochets that are very beautiful and unique. You can make baby shawls using this type of crochet and also throw blankets that are normally used for decoration.

Bruges Crochet

This is a type of crochet that is used when one wants to make Bruges laces—as the name suggests. One first make ribbons for the crochet project, which are sewed together for them to form the desired lace pattern. They are said to form very beautiful patterns that are also unique. This is because they are neatly sewed together. You can use different colors when making these patterns, which makes them even more beautiful. This type of crochet is used for making table mats and shawls, as well as embellishments that are used for clothing.

This is a type of crochet that is said to utilize the stitches that were used traditionally. One uses a very thick yarn when making items using this type of crochet. One has to work on a very thick rope, and since one is making mats, one requires something strong and easy to style and shape. This type of crocheting is mostly used when one is making mats and baskets or anything that is required to be strong. You need to have skills on how to make items using this type of crochet since you need to make first the item that has to be on the ground. This type of crochet is used in the making of mats and baskets as well as wall hangings.

Clones Lace Crochet

This type of crochet was said to be easy to make in the past and was very popular among people who love crocheting. It resembled the Irish lace, which was made because it was so easy to make. Clones knots are made, which are normally part of the crocheting process. You need to learn this skill to ensure you know how to make items using it. This type of crochet is used when one is making delicate dresses that require one to be very keen.

Cro-Hook Crochet

With this type of crochet, one is required to use a hook that is double-sided to be able to achieve crochets that are double-sided. The crocheter is expected to work on an item from both sides, which enables them to come up with a very unique pattern. A crocheter needs to be able to learn this style before using it to make items to get good outcomes from their work. You can make baby clothes and scarves as well as washcloths through this type of crocheting.

Filet Crochet

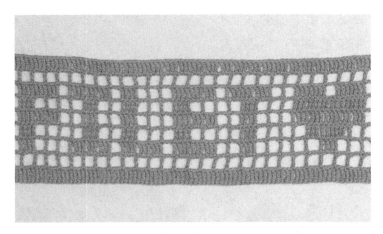

This crochet is a style that is achieved through the use of chains as well as double crochets. One achieves a crochet that has a grid-like pattern, which can be filled or left without filling. The space that is left is used in the creation of desired pictures, which have to be included in the design. It allows for patterns so unique and neatly embedded within the crochet. This is so unique about this type of crochet. All the squares that are left empty when crocheting may be filled with pictures of one desire. With this type of crocheting, you can make baby blankets, handbags, jackets, and kimonos, as well as making cushions.

Finger Crochet

Finger crocheting is practiced when one barely uses the hook when crocheting. It is used when one is making some hand fabrics. In this type of crocheting, you will mostly use your hands to crochet. The patterns are fixed together to come up with one complete item. When one is making fabrics using this type of crochet, one cannot do it too fast. You will spend a lot of time crocheting, resulting in very few items for a very long period. One can only make some string bags and small scarves, which do not require much time to make.

Freeform Crochet

When making this type of crochet, one does not create any pattern on the item. It is very artistic in nature and also very organic. A true crocheter doesn't actually follow any plan, so one can come up with any kind of design they would want. There are, however, people who do not like this type of crochet since they cannot do it without any kind of plan. You need to follow some instructions to be able to make the desired patterns. You can make art pieces using this type of crochet. You can design and make anything you want with this type of crocheting.

Hairpin Crochet

This is a type of crochet that is said to work just like the broomstick crochet, even though in the past people used crochet hooks. Pieces being crocheted were held together through the use of metals there were then. You can use this technique to make very beautiful and well-finished crochet works. You can use it to make shawls and wraps as well as scarves.

Micro Crochet

his type of crocheting is used by modern crocheters. It requires the use of very fine threads and crochet hooks. You have to make sure that they are very careful when using the hooks to ensure that you use them in the right way to make the best types of crochets. You can make teeny tiny things with this technique.

Overly Crochet

Overly crochet is used when one wants to achieve an item that has stitches on top of the item to be able to get a pattern that is raised. You can use more than one color when crocheting, which will enable you to be able to achieve unique and beautiful patterns. You can also make different designs using this type of crochet. You can use this type of crochet when making potholders, wall hangings, and handbags.

Pineapple Crochet

When making items using this type of crochet, one does not follow any given pattern. This is because one can use just one general stitch to shape the desired patterns. You can use it to make scarves and shawls as well as wraps. This type of crochet is not complicated, as anyone can learn it and be able to crochet according to their desired designs.

Chapter 3:
Understanding Patterns

Today are just written instructions, often wrought with abbreviations. Before, in the early days of crochet, patterns were the actual crocheted works of someone else. For example, a lady wanted to crochet a wristband. A written pattern was not available. Instead, she had to get an actual wristband and painstakingly count the stitches and copy them. Then came the scrapbooks. Fragments of crocheted works were sewn on pieces of paper and bound together like a scrapbook. Some had crocheted samples sewn onto larger fabrics, while some were simply kept in a box or bag. Crochet stitch samples were also made in long and narrow bands. In 1824, the earliest crochet pattern was printed. The patterns were for making purses from silver and gold threads.

Early crochet books from the 1800s were small, but they contained a treasury of crochet patterns for lace, bands, lace-like collars, insertions, caps (women's, men's, and children's), purses, and men's slippers. They also contained patterns for white crochet, which were for undergarment trimmings, mats, edgings, and insertions. The books recommended materials such as cotton thread, hemp thread, spool yarn, and linen thread. Colorwork was done in chenille, wool, and silk yarns, with the occasional silver and gold threads.

The problem with these early patterns was their inaccuracy. For example, a crochet pattern could be an 8-point star but would turn out to have only 6 points. These crochet books required the reader to rely more on the illustrations as a better guide.

Today, crochet patterns are more systematic, accurate, and organized. However, to the uninitiated, looking at a crochet pattern is a lot like looking at letters and numbers with no idea of what they mean. Look for the meanings of the abbreviations, which are often printed at the bottom of the pattern. You can research some of the unfamiliar abbreviations.

A crocheter needs to learn the abbreviations, and the symbols used in a crochet pattern. Without this knowledge, there will be a very limited number of patterns a crocheter can work with, as most are written in the crochet language.

Here are a few things to remember when working with patterns:

- Patterns are either made in rounds or rows. The pattern will specify if using either or both. Patterns come with a difficulty rating. Crocheters should choose the level that best suits their abilities. That is, beginners should stick to the pattern that best suits their level while they are still familiarizing themselves with the terms and techniques. Move to higher difficulty levels after gaining enough experience and mastery of the required crochet skills.
- Always count the stitches made while working and then after reaching the end of the row or round.

- Always check the gauge, especially if the project has to turn out the exact size and shape as indicated in the pattern.
- Learning to read crochet patterns requires practice and experience. Be patient and don't get annoyed.

How to Read a Crochet Pattern

Crochet patterns would often only list the abbreviations and the number of stitches required for each row or round. Some patterns would also use abbreviations for other instructions, such as when to turn or when to begin and end.

The simplest crochet pattern would look like this:

Row 1: Use a size E crochet hook, ch15, single crochet 2nd ch from hook, and for each ch, turn. (14 single crochet).

This can look more like a foreign language for beginners. This is still the simplest of crochet patterns. Translated, the line means:

Row 1: With a crochet hook size E, make 15 chain stitches. Starting on the 2nd stitch from the hook, make a single crochet stitch across the chain stitches. Then make a turning stitch. By the end of the row, there should be 12 single crochet stitches done.

Circle Patterns

Circles are also common in crochet. It starts with a center ring, which is the foundation of all rounds, as the foundation chain work in rows. The center ring is created either by making a ring from chain stitches or from a single chain stitch. The first method creates a hole in the middle of the circle crochet work. The second method has an inconspicuous center.

Working with a Hole as a Center Ring

This is the most common way of making a center ring. A row of chain stitches is created, then it is looped off to make a ring. The hole in the middle is determined by how many chain stitches were made at the beginning. It also determines how many stitches can be made through the center ring. Avoid making the chain stitch too long because the resulting ring would be too large and unsteady.

Ch6 (make 6 chain stitches).

Place the crochet hook into the 1st chain stitch, the one farthest from the crochet hook, and next to the slip knot. This will now form a ring.

Do 1 yarn over (yo).

Pull the yarn through the chain stitch and through the loop resting on the crochet hook. This completes the center ring with a hole visible in the middle.

Working with a hole for a center is easy because the stitches are made by going through the center hole instead of into the actual chain stitches of the ring.

From the finished center ring above, make ch1 as a turning chain to be used for the single crochet of the first row.

Place the crochet hook through the center ring.

Make 1 yo. Pull the wrapped yarn all the way through the hole (center ring).

Make another yo and pull it through the 2 loops resting in the crochet hook. This finishes with 1 single crochet (single crochet).

Continue making single crochet through the center hole until it can't fit anymore.

Working with the Chain Stitch

This is another way of working in rounds. This is used when the pattern calls for a very small or barely noticeable center hole. Generally, one starts with a slipknot and ch1, then one adds the number of chain stitches required for a turning chain. For example, make 1 chain stitch then another 3 if using double crochet, because the turning chains for dc are 3 chain stitches.

CH1

If using double crochet (dc), make ch3.

Perform 1 yarn over and place the hook into the center of the 4th chain stitch from the hook. This is the 1st ch made and is located next to the slipknot.

Make 1 double crochet into this chain stitch. Continue making dc on the other chain stitches. For beginners, a crochet pattern might look like it's written in a completely different language, and in a way, it is. Designers and crocheters use a language of abbreviations and conventions that are standardized, making it easy for anyone who understands this language to follow a pattern. The following is a breakdown of the most common ways the information used in a crochet pattern—and what it all means.

Materials

This usually includes the yarn, hook size, and any extra items. Sometimes patterns include the brand names of yarn or other items, but sometimes they merely contain the type of material needed (Lion Brand Fishermen's Wool Yarn versus 100 percent worsted weight yarn, for example).

Gauge

Gauge is a dreaded word to even experienced crocheters, but it doesn't have to be. Putting it simply, the gauge is the measurement of the number of crochet stitches and rows per inch of fabric. Why is this important? Because achieving the proper gauge ensures that the finished item will turn out the correct size. Ignore gauge—and what is supposed to be a cropped—and snug cardigan might become a housedress.

A pattern will indicate gauge either over 1 inch or 4 inches of stitches. For example, a gauge section might indicate, "3 stitches and 4 rows over 1 inch in single crochet." This means that if the crocheter works a fabric in single crochet, he or she should have 3 stitches and 4 rows in every inch.

Before beginning a project, the crocheter checks that they are getting gauges by crocheting at least a 4-inch by 4-inch swatch in the pattern stitch, then blocking it, and measuring it carefully. If the gauge matches the size of the crochet project, it's okay to start the project. If the gauge does not match it, the crocheter needs to change either the hook size or the yarn until they get the proper gauge. This is necessary because small differences in gauge can equal big differences in a finished item—a row of 30 single crochet stitches at 3 stitches per inch will be 10 inches long, whereas a row of 30 single crochet at 4 stitches per inch will only be 7.5 inches long—not an unimportant difference.

The crocheter should generally change the hook size before changing the yarn. If the gauge is smaller than required (e.g., 2 stitches per inch instead of 3), the hook is too large. If the gauge is larger than required (e.g., 4 stitches per inch instead of 3), the hook is too small. Gauge is much more adaptable in crochet, but the crocheter should still aim to get the gauge right of both.

Note that with some projects, a gauge is more important than with others. For items with a lot of shaping, including sweaters, mittens, socks, and hats, a gauge is critical. For items that are more 'one size fits all,' a small difference in gauge might be okay—a scarf that is an inch wider than the design intended isn't necessarily the end of the world.

Abbreviations

Many times, this includes instructions for working special stitches. If a crocheter doesn't understand some of the stitches used in the pattern, the abbreviations are a good place to look for help. Many abbreviations are standardized, so as crocheters gain practice reading patterns, they learn to immediately recognize single crochet for single crochet, dc for double crochet, and so on.

Instructions

The instructions are the meat of the pattern, the place where the designer tells the crocheter what to do to make the item. For the most part, designers are explicit, for example, "Chain 3, work 3 for turning chain, double crochet into the third chain from hook," but a few common shortcuts are used as well, including:

Asterisks

Asterisks are used to indicate repeats of patterns. A pattern might indicate, "Chain 1, slip stitch into the second chain from hook, *3 single crochet, ch 2, 3 single crochet*, repeat from * to * three times, chain 1, turn." The stitches within the asterisks are repeated three times in the sequence they're given after the first time they're worked. So, in total, the asterisk would be repeated four times.

Parentheses

Parentheses are used to indicate repeats, often within asterisks. The crocheter might indicate, "...*3 single crochet, (ch 2, single crochet) twice, 3single crochet*, repeat from * to * three times." To work the directions inside the asterisks, the crocheter would work 3 single crochet, 2 chains, 1 single crochet, 2 chains, 1 single crochet, then 3 more single crochet. Then the crocheter would repeat the instructions inside the asterisks the number of times called for.

Many crochet patterns are also broken down into rows (for flat crochet) and rounds (for circular crochet). Pattern repeats are often made up of many rows or rounds, which the designer will indicate in the pattern. At the end of the pattern, the designer will include any special finishing instructions, such as how to add embellishments or borders.

New crocheters should remember that although these are common conventions used in crochet, there are exceptions, as designers are individuals, and some have their own unique way of writing instructions.

Chapter 4:
Materials Needed for Crochet

Here are the basic materials for starting up a crochet project:

- Yarn
- Crochet hook
- Scissors
- Darning needle
- Tape measure
- Hook organizer
- Stitch markers
- Row counter
- Stitch patterns
- Crochet material organizer

The materials help in one way or another in making crochet. However, for beginners, one can use the basic ones.

Yarn

Yarn is a thread used in sewing or knitting any form of material. This is the backbone of crochet. It is the only material that comes out of the final product as it carries everything from designing to the conclusion. For beginners, it is advised to use a medium-weight yarn as it is easy to crawl it with the hooks.

There are different types of yarns according to your preference, and it is better to understand them before buying them. The common material is polyester and wool. There is also nylon, acrylic, rayon, and viscose, which can be the best choice according to one's preference.

Here are the types of yarns:

- Natural fibers
- Synthetic fibers
- Eco-friendly fibers

Natural Fibers: These are yarns made from natural materials.

Cotton: This is a material harvested from cotton plants a process is used to preserve them to last longer.

Silk: This is a form of material made from the larvae of silkworms and is mostly incorporated with other fibers to create a neat and long-lasting yarn.

Cashmere: Just from its name, you can see it is drawn from a cashmere goat and is known for being soft and warm at the same time.

Linen: This is harvested from a flash plant and is commonly used for light garments.

Wool This is so common in clothes and yarn, and it is a perfect material for heavy yarns.

Synthetic Fibers: As stated above, this is the commonly preferred material for yarn and is among the selling materials in the world. This includes nylon, polyester, acrylic, rayon, and viscose.

Organic Cotton: This is cotton made from cotton plants and is not treated with chemicals.

Bamboo: Bamboo has always been used to make products for different uses and its silk is harvested as it makes a perfect yarn because of its strength.

Those are just a sample of the commonly used yarns, which are formed from different fibers for different types of crochets according to users' needs.

Hooks

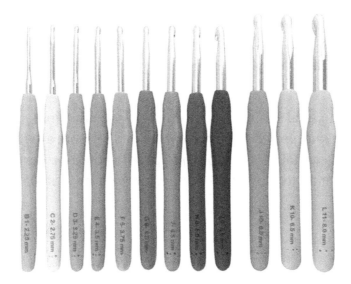

These are primarily the needles used to hook up and do stitching on yarn to form crochet. The hook drives the yarn on each one in a back-and-forth manner to form beautiful crochet. Sometimes, it is used concurrently with needles when a misstep is made on crochet.

Hooks come in different sizes, and it is better to choose a perfect one depending on the yarns' sizes and design. It is advisable to always consider all this before starting up, for some hooks may not perfectly fit your desired project.

Scissors

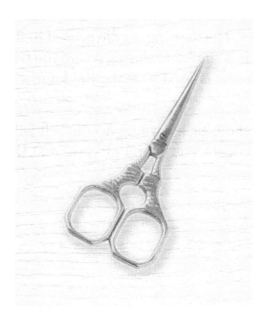

This is a tool commonly used in homesteads for homemade clothes or trimming oversized curtains and towels. It is also known for being used by tailors for cutting their materials and other trimmings of textile. Scissors on crochet are also paramount.

Just like the hooks, there are different types of scissors, with different functions useful for crochet. The basic one is the general craft scissors, which can be found locally and easily. It is okay to use the general craft scissors on different fibers because it does not leave sharp edges, and it cuts in a zigzag manner just like the pinking shears. Here, the type of scissors does matter when the crochet is in the completion stage, as it helps cut it into nice pieces without producing, without tearing the yarns, threads, or fabrics.

When buying them online, make sure you check their specifications, as certain types of scissors might not be suitable for your project. The recommended scissors are standard, snips, embroidery scissors, and lastly the dressmaker. Embroidery scissors could be perfect for this case because it helps cut the exact yarn being used without tampering with the rest of the project.

Darning Needle

As the name suggests, it is a form of a needle with a bigger hole than the normal needle where the yarn passes through. The sharp end is a little blunt compared to a sewing needle and helps in making a perfect end on crochet. The darning needle is used to fix the end of each crochet so that it can be steady when in use. This is similar to sewing where you tie a knot at the end of the material, but for crochet, the darning needle is used to make the knot which will keep the whole crochet intact and in perfect shape.

There is no big problem when choosing a darning needle is it will fit the crochet project. The one with a larger hole can accommodate every kind of yarn, and there should not be any problem whatsoever.

Stitch Markers

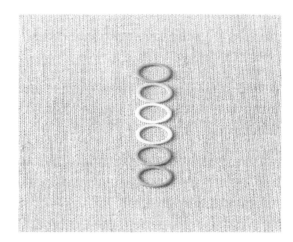

These are clips used to mark areas of interest in crochet. There are different designs of crochets and when you have a slightly complex craft; it is always advisable for one to have a stitch marker. For beginners, it is always complicated to make crochets with corners or even rounded by following the pattern. This means the stitch markers are perfect for making areas where it forms patterns unless one is a professional.

Stitch makers have crafted clips that help indicate or put marks on a design to help a beginner or a craftsman to have a perfect and uniformed crotchet.

Any size and type of stitch markers can be used on any piece and type of yarn, as it does not favor the material. The maker can be found in local stores and most people prefer them depending on the sizes of their hands, or how perfectly they can hold them.

Tape Measure

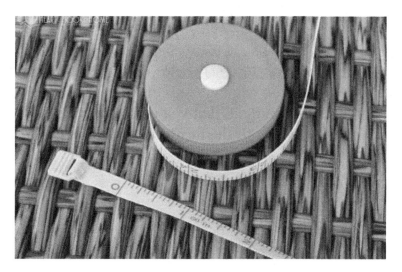

Some of you could be wondering why almost everything that is used by tailors is being used to craft crochet, and the answer is yes, it needs to be totally perfect. Tailors are always seen with tape measures and to make crochet, you might want to get one too, especially for a beginner. The tape

31

measure is simply for measuring and making the right adjustments when following a designed pattern.

This is a necessary tool when there is clipping using stitch markers, as it will help to create uniform patterns and with minimal or no blundering.

However, for crochet flowers, this might not be necessary as they are very simple and can be modified easily, but it is advisable for big projects and to avoid disappointments at the end of it with different and unorganized sizes.

Tape measures also come in different sizes and types and other specifications, depending on the country you are located in. For a clear understanding, make sure you get a tape measure that supports your form of measurements. For instance, America's measurement is different from Russia's and the United Kingdom's. To make perfect measurements, beware of the measurements placed as some may be misleading or have different calculations depending on their form of measurements.

Row Counters

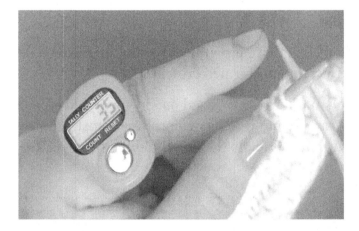

Row counters are invaluable when you start to crochet. They will help you keep your place when you are working on a project, and they genuinely help you stay on the right track, so you don't get lost between the rows. Essentially, row counters are little chains that you loop onto your crochet hook, and they have little numbers on them that you can move to track your row progress while working. After every row, you move up to the next number in the chain, so you don't lose your progress.

Hook Organizer

After making the first and second patterns, you get to know the stitch patterns and designs that can work for you as you continue to be creative and innovative. The hook organizer resembles a car toolbox, and is always referred to as "do it yourself" and can work on your car anytime, anywhere. For the crochet, this is almost similar as it carries your essential materials for the work.

After finishing the work, the hook organizer helps keep all the materials used as it has pocket-like spaces for placing hooks, tape measures, darning needles, yarn, and other combinations of crochet tools. One can make any design that can hold the materials with ease and keep them in order. Instead of buying a toolbox for such materials, make one to place crochet projects in and you will be shocked at how you continue to perfect your craft.

Chapter 5:
Right-Handed Crocheters

Wherever you look, whoever you ask about starting your crochet career, the answer will be the same—the very base of your crochet is the chain, and almost every crochet pattern begins with a chain. If working in rounds or working granny squares, you need to make five chains in a row and join them so that you create a circle. All subsequent squares will be worked in that circle to start shaping your crochet.

How do you create a chain? First, you must form a slip knot. In most crochet projects, the first step is making the slip knot. Again, when it comes to slip knots, there are many ways to make them. We will examine one of the easiest ways. First, twist a loose loop of yarn onto the hook. Hold the tail of the yarn between your thumb and index finger. Use the rest of your fingers to control the yarn that keeps unwinding from the ball. Draw the yarn into the loop with your crochet hook. Tighten the loose slip knot that is now on your hook. Remember not to tighten it too much. Make sure your crochet hook can move easily in the loop. Now, start the chain to make progress.

You hold your slip knot with a hook, now wrap the yarn over the loop and pull it through to make a new loop. You have made your first chain stitch. To make more chain stitches, make another loop and draw the yarn through. You can repeat this as much as needed for your project.

When you have five chains, you can join them to form a circle. As we said before, all the stitches will be worked in that circle. Once the chain is done, you need to join the circle. This is done by putting the crochet hook through the first stitch, the wool around the hook, and pulling it through. This leaves you ready to commence with the first row.

There is no point to change colors at this stage. You are doing your first chain, your first circle. It's better to try more difficult experimentations with color later. But if you really want to change colors, you must cut the wool and pull it through the final loop so that it is tightly fastened. However, by following the guide step by step with the stitches, you'll need to keep the wool attached, so you will not be able to change colors.

Now you learned the basics—holding your crochet hook and making a chain and a circle to work with. You can increase the number of chains as much as you want to make a larger circle if you want to or need to. When working on a flat item, opposed to one that is worked in rounds, you will need to work across instead of into a circle, thus building your crochet work. How to make a sweater? Merely continue by adding rows, keeping the sides as straight as possible until shaping is required.

Basic Crochet Stitches for Beginners

Having learned how to make a chain, now it's important to understand that the chain is not used only as casting on, but it is also used to create shapes or the corners for granny squares. By the end of this guide, you will have learned how to use chains for those purposes. Now we will take a deep look into the ways to create different stitches and the most common stitches in crochet, giving you the ability to work from patterns.

Single Crochet

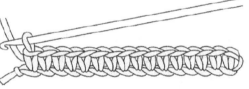

Final result

The single crochet is the most found stitch and the easiest one to make. Easy and fast. It is good for creating shaped items like jackets or skirts. It is also good for decorating finished work as it creates a tight and dense fabric. You can use this stitch alone repeatedly or together with other stitches. It is the most fundamental of all stitches. Below is how to use single crochet:

1. First, prepare a series of chains, then insert your hook on the SECOND chain facing you and your yarn.
2. Wrap the yarn towards you with your crochet hook. Remember to wrap it from back to front (wrap the yarn from the back to the front—this is called "yarn over" or "yo"). At this point, pull the hook. If all have been done properly, you are supposed to have two loops to work with.

3. Pass the yarn through the two loops, and you will have completed your first single crochet. Repeat the operation until you finish all the chains.
4. To continue, put your hook onto the next chain stitch and repeat all the operations from step two to complete the second stitch and so on.

We were talking about chain circles before. We can practice the single crochet stitch with the circle. Place the crochet hook into the circle. Put the wool over the hook. Place the wool around and pull it through the two loops on your hook (we went through this before) to form a single crochet stitch. Carry on repeating the same process until you have worked for all the circles.

When you get to the other side of the circle, join the circle up by placing the hook through the first single crochet that you made, wrap the wool over the hook, and pull through both stitches on the hook. To tie off, cut off the wool and then pull it through the loop on your hook. This time, pull tight to fasten.

Double Crochet

Double crochet is the second basic stitch that you need to learn. It is one of the most useful, if not the ultimate useful stitch in crocheting. Once you have mastered it, you can put it to use in creating sweaters, shawls, afghans, home and celebrations décor, and lots of other projects.

We start with our already worked circle.

Insert your crochet hook into the desired stitch. Yarn over your hook (YA) and rotate the hook towards you. With the wrapped yarn, pull the hook through the stitch. At this point, you should have two loops on the hook. YA again and draw the hook with the wrapped yarn into both loops on your hook.

You have now created one double crochet (U.K. style). If all is OK, there should be one unstitched loop on the hook. Repeat.

Double crochet is explained in different ways by different experts from different countries. More often than not, there are differences even between experts from the same country. It is such a basic stitch that it cannot have a single description of how to make it. It is always better to hear different opinions, to understand them properly.

For example, double stitches can be explained as below from a USA expert:

"Start a new chain and join it so that you are ready to try a new stitch. The stitch is a little larger than a single crochet. Place the crochet hook into a circle and wind wool around the hook for the start of the next stitch. Repeat the stitch outlined in bold above until you have a complete circle then join off the circle as before."

Two ways to explain the same thing—the fun is to find what matches you.

Treble Crochet

Continuing our journey through the main stitches, it is time to learn the treble crochet. Treble crochet is another key basic stitch that you are likely to need for several crochet projects. Trebles can either stand-alone or, like all other basic stitches, can be fused with other ones to make pleasing stitch patterns. Trebles are versatile and can be used in every way imaginable. They also work in numerous configurations, such as triangles, circles, squares, rows, and many other shapes. You can use them in almost any thread or yarn, which means you can try practically any material. No need to say that new material must be experimented with in a later stage of your learning experience.

You can begin your crocheting from a starting chain. Alternatively, there are many ways you can get started. We will consider the start of our work from a chain for now.

Instructions

Your chain should be 3 more chains than the number of triple stitches the pattern needs.

Skip the first 4 chains, they are turning chains. Your hook is already through the single loop you have in your chain. YA twice. Insert the hook from the front to the back of the work into the center of the fifth chain (having skipped four, remember?). YO through the chain. You should have four loops on your hook now (see image below).

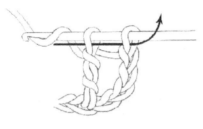

One treble crochet

YO and draw it through the two loops currently on the hook (3 loops still on the hook). YO and draw it through two loops on hook (2 loops remaining on hook). Yarn over, draw yarn through the remaining loops on the hook, and you've completed one triple crochet (see image below).

YO twice, insert the hook into the middle of the next stitch, YO, and draw it through the stitch (YO, draw through loops on hook) 3 times. Repeat until you get to the end of the chain. Now you are ready to begin the second row.

To begin, you must turn in your work. Start by chaining four (turning chain). Skip the first treble (we talked about it in the beginning). YO twice. On the next triple crochet, insert the hook from the front to the back under the top 2 loops and repeat 3 times. Your first triple crochet is now done. Repeat this step in each treble until you reach the end.

Treble crochet

The image shows what your work should look like when you are working on a flat item rather than a rounded one.

Using Different Stitches to Their Best Advantages

The best way to get accustomed to the different stitches you have learned is to make a sampler. You can begin with a chain of whatever length you like. The most common and more typical are chains of 25 links for a small sample, but it is totally up to you.

Create a chain and then work one row of double crochet stitches. Turn the work around and work another row of double crochet stitches, ten trebles for two rows. Follow this with working into every third hole and creating three trebles into one hole before working on the next third hole to make your next group of trebles. Trebles are very suitable for grouping work. You can try different block groupings.

Typical sampler

Do two rows for all the designs that you decide to experiment with. This provides you with a clearer image of what you can produce using that stitch. You can always refer to your sampler when you are making something if you need to verify how you achieved something. Most experts create samplers in multi-colored wool so they can clearly see the stitches. It takes a little longer, but it's worth the time.

Decreasing and Increasing

When you make the garment, you will need to decrease and increase to make the shape of the pieces that form the garment. As usual in crochet, what you must do is much easier than you might imagine.

To increase a crochet, just increase the stitches in the same hole, which makes the current row have more stitches than the last.

Decreasing is done by working as shown in the diagram below. The image is better than the description. However, it is worth it to spend some time describing how to decrease.

To decrease the crochet pattern, you make the pattern normally but omit the last part of the stitch, leaving the worked loops on your hook. You then work the next stitch as usual, with the last stitch's loop still on your hook. In the end, you pull your hook through all the loops to combine them together.

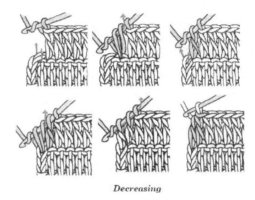

Decreasing

Although you might consider the above as very complex, it isn't. Like most of the other stitches, it is easier to do it than to explain how to do it.

Chapter 6:
Left-Handed Crocheters

Being a left-handed crocheter is a unique thing because you will operate against the current status quo of things. This is due to the fact left-handed crocheters have to draw their knowledge from right-handed crocheters. Thinking about this is a little bit hard for left-handed crocheters. You can imagine learning a skill from an individual who does not have an understanding of it. Well, that's in the past.

Today, the situation is different, as left-handed crocheters have a vast number of sources from where they can draw knowledge from. These sources include various tutorials, patterns, and teachers who have brought themselves to spread the mastery of this art.

When we talk about left-handed crocheting, this is almost as mimicking right-handed crocheting. This is because left-handed crocheting borrows a lot from right-handed crocheting. It can almost seem like a reflection of the other.

The left-handed crocheter, just as the name suggests, will hold his or her crochet on the left hand while the right-handed one will make sure that the crochet is on his or her right-hand side. There are various grips that one may use when holding the hook. This includes the knife grip or the pencil grip. When this happens, the crocheter may manipulate the hook in whichever way he or she desires.

With left-handed crochet, learning the basics and following the patterns of crocheting is subtle. This is because they are going out of their way to learn the mastery of what they have not been doing daily. Moreover, many crocheting patterns follow the direction of right-handed patterns.

To make this less subtle for you as a left-handed crocheter, you need to learn the basis of left-handed crocheting. Below are the various steps which can be very helpful when beginning left-handed crocheting or when maintaining its perfection.

The Hook Should Be in Your Left Hand

Crocheting left-handed will mean you will have to put the crochet in your left hand. This way, your right hand will have the leeway to support the work that you are manipulating. The hook has a flat part that is key when manipulating your work. When you are performing the task, your thumb and finger should be on the grip of the flat part of the hook. Holding the crochet properly is key when it comes to effective sewing. The grip of the crochet should be maintained and balanced all through your sewing.

Chaining

The foundation of crocheting begins with this stage. When you are engaging in a crochet project for the first time, you will need to practice chaining. One of the less subtle techniques in crocheting is this one. To achieve this, you need to start by making sure you loop the yarn on your finger. This is often done twice. Your finger here meaning the index finger. After you have achieved this, the next step will be that you will gently pull your second loop through the first loop.

The result of this is what we call a slip stitch. After this is achieved, you will need to make sure that you slide the loop that is on your hook. After this, you free the end of the yarn over the hook. To make another loop, you need to slide a novel yarn through the loop that was already inexistent.

To make sure that the number of chains is increasing, you need to carry out this activity in a continuous manner. This way, you will find that you have achieved a chain. Forming a chain is the most basic stance of crocheting since you are carrying out this activity in a continuous manner. The chain should only be limited to the purposes of your project. When in decreasing, chaining is often referred to by the abbreviation "ch."

Slip Stitching

A slip stitch, as it is known, can also be referred to as a stitch that is jointed. The process of slip stitching is one that involves the insertion of the hook through the stitch. Once this has been achieved, you will need to proceed to yarn over. To complete the formation of the slip stitch, you will need to make sure that the novel yarn passes through the stitch. With this at hand, you have accomplished the slip stitch. With a slip-stitch, you can be able to move from one point to another. It can also be used as a link between two stitches. Linking two stitches is of key importance, for instance, when you are making around while crocheting.

Single Crochet

This is a type of stitch which comes as a result of patterns. To achieve this type of stitch, you will first need to make sure that the hook goes through the stitch and then make sure that the yarn passes through both stitches. After you have accomplished this, you will need to make sure your yarn is over. This then involves the yarn being pulled through both loops in a bid to hook it. When abbreviating a single stitch of crochet, this is often denoted as "sc."

Double Crochet

After you have achieved a single crochet, the next step will involve that you do a double crochet. These are other types of crochets that are also common. When double crocheting, you will need to yarn over twice to bring about the double effect. Yarning the second time will involve that you insert the hook through the stitch first before you make a yarn. Double crochet is denoted by "dc."

Half-Double Crochet

This type of stitch is not commonly known. Despite this, we must get to know this type of stitch. This is because when engaging in a type of work that is more complex in nature, you will need to employ the use of this particular type of stitch. To achieve this type of stitch, you need to yarn over, after which you then make sure that the hook goes into the stitch. After you have achieved this, you will need to yarn once more, but this time you are pulling through some stitches. It could be three. Half double crochet is often denoted as "hdc."

Triple Crochet

With knowledge of single and double crochet in mind, you will now need to focus on acquiring the knowledge of triple crochet. In order to achieve a triple crochet, your first move will be to yarn over twice. This way, you are in a position to make sure that the hook goes into the stitch and that you can yarn over once more.

After you have achieved this, you will need to pull this yarn through the existing four loops. With this in place, you will further need to pull the hook over through two loops, after which you will then have to yarn once more. To finish the stitch, you will have to consider pulling through the final two loops. When denoting this type of stitch, you will do so in a manner that suggests the formation of a "tr."

Circle Crochet

When carrying out this particular type of stitch as a left-handed, it will follow the same path as it would when you are right-handed. We have already gathered how to make a chain, which will be your first order of events. To crochet in a circle, you will first need to make a chain. You have already gathered how a slip stitch works, and so after you have achieved a chain, you will need to gather it at the center by using a slip stitch. When you have already achieved this, you are in a position to advance in your chain-making. Circle crochet is an effective way to make heavy scarfs, cowls, and hats.

Try Out Various Special Stitches

When crocheting, you can make different patterns that come in handy when you want to create something captivating. We have already had a feel of what basic stitches entail, and to comprehend more complex stitches, we will first need to have an understanding of the basic stitches. Apart from the basic stitches, we have already gathered, there exist other types of stitches that come in handy when creating something interesting. These types of stitches include pop-corn stitch, box stitch, and shell stitch.

As a left-handed, there are several things that will stand out when seeking and catch up with apt crocheting. Some of these factors include:

Left-Handed Tutorials

Crocheting is a practical venture. When indulging in crocheting for the first time, you will need to have as much practical assistance as possible. With reference pictures, you are in a position to effectively understand the formation of a particular type of stitch. This is because you can see it as it forms. Learning how to crochet is an uphill task, especially for left-handed individuals. The internet is full of a lot of tutorials on crocheting using the left hand. An individual may use this when seeking out crocheting. With a tutorial, you are blowing to follow through the whole process of crocheting all the way to your success.

This is because you can pause and rewind where you might not have done correctly. Moreover, there are blogs of other left-handed crocheters in existence. Following them and acquiring knowledge from them is easier because they tend to relate to you. There are also left-handed crocheters books. These books are various in the market, and thus you can choose to settle on one that works best for you.

Following the Pattern to the Letter

Left-handed crocheting entails that you encompass the same patterns that a right-handed crocheter would use. When you have a pattern for right-handed crocheters, you will follow the pattern to the letter, only using your left hand when doing this. This also means that you can use many right-handed tutorials to your advantage.

You may be watching a tutorial for right-handed crocheters, but when you follow through with your left hand, you will find that you achieve the same results. And as a result, you find that right-handed crocheters and left-handed crocheters are the same. The only distinction is that one uses the right hand, whereas the other uses the help of his or her left hand.

Flipping Pictures and Images

Most left-handed individuals refrain from right-handed tutorials not because The tutorials cannot work for benefit of them, but because of their already formed perception about this kind of tutorials. To make sure this perception is eradicated from left-handed individuals. A left-handed crocheter ought to practice patterns and ways that will work to their advantage. One of the most tactful procedures a left-handed may adopt in a bid to secure a deeper comprehension of patterns is by taking them and inverting them. When you invert a picture that was taken by a right-handed individual, you will find that it appears as if it is from a left-handed individual. There are several points to note when dealing with left-handed crocheting. For instance, you need to leave your beginning yarning tail hanging. This should be done at the beginning of every project; its essence is deep-rooted to the instance that you should not crochet over it. The tails come in handy when creating a cue, whether you are on the right-hand side of the cue or the left-hand side.

The right side always manifests itself at the right bottom corner. Another point to note if you are a left-handed crocheter is that every time you are adopting a position of yarning over, you are doing this in a clockwise manner. You need to master this move as this is what makes sense to the whole process of crocheting.

There are numerous patterns for left-handed crocheters; this may involve the written ones and also the visible ones that are visual. Although the visible ones seem easier, left-handed crocheting is possible for both types of crocheting.

A pattern that has been written down can easily be followed through just by the use of cognitive awareness that, for left-handed, the direction of the yarn will be a little different. There are various types of patterns that, to work best, need to be reversed, so they can be implemented with ease. For instance, there is a type of crochet pattern known as the tapestry pattern that requires reversing for it to work properly. There are also other patterns known as colorwork patterns that require a reversal for them to function properly.

When you reverse filet crochet, one that is used when writing words, you are in a position to read the letters that were written in a manner that is reversed. When a left-handed does not work on reversing this particular type of work, you will find that this creates confusion on the rows and the stitches.

Often, the expected outcome will not arrive because of the mismatch in the various rows and stitches. With symbol charts, this is directed to right-handed crochets. Owing to this fact, left-handed crocheters ought to follow the same drill as depicted in the symbol charts, but in a manner that is opposing to the already depicted symbol.

This means that you will adopt the symbol but in an opposite manner. Reversing a pattern can be done in the consciousness of an individual. This entails the individual forming a picture in his or her head and in turn, reversing it. If you cannot do this, the best way to reverse the pattern would be by using a mirror.

Chapter 7:
Tips and Tricks for Crocheting

Below are some tips and tricks for crocheting:

- To avoid balls of yarn from falling and rolling, place them in reused hand wipe jar of cylindrical shape. Just like wipes, the yarn will also come out through the same hole.
- Mark your rows by using a stitch marker, bobby pin, or safety pin.
- Store your crochet hooks in a jewelry box, pencil box, or travelling toothpaste holder. You can also hang your hooks on a small piece of wool. A multipurpose storage box is also a good option.
- Highlight your pattern with different colors so that you can understand it easily. Underline different stitches. If your patterns demand rows of a different color, highlight the rows with the same color or with the colors that you have decided to use.
- Always keep abbreviations, measurements, hook, and yarn weights table in printable forms so that you can easily use them whenever you want.
- Use leftover yarns to make pom poms, Afghan squares, bracelets, and many more articles like these.
- If you use homespun yarn for your pattern, then metal hooks are a better option than plastic ones.
- If you love to do crochet during travelling, prepare a separate crochet box. Always have travel-friendly crochet tools, for example, foldable scissors that are easy to carry and also will not snug the things in the bag.
- Many crochet patterns do not go well with ironing. So instead of it, take an equal quantity of water and starch and spray the pattern with it, and let it dry on a flat surface.
- Store the crochet patterns in your notebook by using sheet protectors.
- Make sure you sit in a proper position to provide enough support to your elbows, and hands during crocheting.
- Take breaks after regular intervals to refresh yourself.
- There is a variety of hand massage and stretching techniques. So, do the ones you find easy to relax your hand muscles.
- Using ergonomic crochet tools such as circular needles is also useful to avoid hand fatigue.
- Use stress relief gloves.
- Pick up your hook every day. The hardest part about learning how to crochet is training your hand to hold your hook (and the yarn) with the correct tension. At first, it feels a little awkward and unnatural but if you make it a habit of picking up your hook every day when you are first learning the craft. It will become easy in no time. Do not give up and keep in mind that practice makes perfect!

- Begin with small projects. Learning how to crochet takes time and most of the time, beginners feel discouraged when they are not able to complete a project—I mean, who wouldn't? The best thing to do is to start with small attainable projects. There is no better feeling than completing your very own first project. Start with small items such as squares, mandalas, and coasters before moving onto larger projects such as blankets and cushions.
- Chain, chain, chain. When learning to crochet, making several chains is the best way to improve your skills, since they are the foundation of all stitches. You will be ready for stitches that are more complicated once all your chains look nice and even.
- Make stitch swatches. You can work on small swatches to help you to familiarize yourself with the different stitches. You can even sew these swatches together to create face cloths or small blankets.
- Avoid changing hooks in the middle of a project. Your stitches should be consistent throughout the whole project. When you switch hooks mid-project, you risk creating an inconsistency. Even changing the same size hooks from one manufacture to another can be problematic. This is because the size of the hook is not always the same between manufacturers and a small change in how the hooks are shaped can change the way you make your stitches or hold the hook—hence the need for practice swatches.

Mistakes and Solutions in Crocheting

As a beginner, you must come across your fair share of frustrations as you get stuck in your crocheting. Mistakes could happen by not following instructions accurately, or simply as a result of practice. Remember, there are certain methods you can adjust slightly to suit you, as long as they don't affect the appearance of your stitches and your pattern.

Learning to crochet can be a wonderful experience, so try not to get too despondent if you don't always manage to do everything properly at first. It is a very time-consuming craft and requires a lot of skill, which you will develop over time. Don't be too hard on yourself and just have fun.

Perhaps you may not be familiar with some of this, depending on how much crocheting you have done up to this point. Go through them and keep them in mind if you ever have any of these challenges in the future.

Inserting Your Hook into the Wrong Chain When You Start

Don't count the first chain on the hook because it is just a loop; your first proper chain is the first chain from the hook, which is the one next to and the one after that is the second loop on the hook.

Using US Stitches When Your Pattern Contains UK pattern Terms

This can sometimes be really easy to miss and cause several complications. An easy way to check is to look out for single crochet instruction as this confirms that your pattern is a US pattern that uses US terminology.

Not Considering Blocking as an Important Step

First of all, blocking involves handwashing an item and then pinning it into place on a blocking mat. The reason for doing this is to straighten the item and flatten it if needed. It is possible to machine-wash your item, just use the hand setting. There are times when blocking isn't completely necessary, whereas so for you. If you intend to wash your crochet item, then be sure to use the blocked gauge measurements.

Making Starting Loops Using Linked Chains and Not a Magic Loop

You could use methods of starting your crocheting in a circle. The first is to work four or five chain stitches and join them in a circle by using a slip stitch. This is the simplest method.

However, a more effective method is to start loops using a magic circle. The center of the circle is much tighter than that of a regular circle linked by a chain stitch. The important thing to remember is consistency. If you use motifs on any items, only use one method to create them as your work will be tidier. So, try them both and see which one you are more comfortable with using and stick to that method.

Not Changing the Size of Your Hook as Needed

You may have done this and only realized it when your work didn't look quite right. This can happen when your starting chain is rather tight in comparison to the rest of your work. This is, however, a common mistake among beginners. You must have the right tension in your chain as it forms the foundation of your work.

One solution is to use a hook slightly larger than recommended in your pattern, as this will help you to have a more even tension throughout. It is not necessary to change the size of your hook if the tension of your work is correct. Always be aware of specific crochet hook sizes on your patterns.

Your Work Seems to Be Shrinking

If you find that your work is shrinking in places and the shape of your item doesn't look right, then you have probably made an error somewhere. The explanation for a mistake such as this is usually a result of making your first stitch in the incorrect position.

Remember these points:

- For a single crochet, the first stitch is inserted into the first stitch of the row above.
- For your other basic stitches, it is the turning chain that is to be counted as the first stitch. Hence, this first stitch is inserted into what is the second one of the previous rows.

Not Being Able to Identify Your Stitches

It is common for beginners to be so involved in trying to follow the instructions in their patterns that they seldom check to see whether their stitches actually look the way they should. Never fear, this is quite normal, and a mistake made by so many of us. There are lots of different moving parts, and it takes a while to adapt your rhythm.

Avoiding New Techniques Because They Seem Too Difficult

If something seems too difficult, look at it more carefully before avoiding it completely. If you can do the basic stitches, you'll be able to handle nearly all the crochet techniques without any problem. You may just need to practice a few times. The steps can sometimes seem a bit intimidating, but if you read through them, you'll see that they are made up of basic instructions. So, don't avoid trying something new, it may be easier than you think, and you'll be able to take your crochet to a new level before you know it!

Not Learning Enough About Yarn

When you start buying yarns, learn as much as you can about them. You will, of course, have to use certain yarns depending on the patterns you are making. But also try to find out which ones are of good quality and don't always go for the cheapest.

You don't realize that your turning chain is the same height as the first stitch in the row.

You should be able to see that starting a chain of your row brings the height of your work up to that of the first stitch in that row. For example, single crochet is one chain, and half double crochet is two chains. Have a look at this the next time you are crocheting.

Not Being Able to Read Patterns

Nowadays, one can tend to be a little bit lazy when it comes to reading patterns. This is because online videos are much quicker and easier to follow for some of us. However, this is not ideal, as one should be able to read patterns. By reading through the pattern steps, you'll be able to create a picture in your mind of what the pattern should look like, and it will give you a better understanding of what you are doing.

Not Learning Corner-to-Corner (C2C) Crochet

The C2C method is an important and useful one to learn. You will most definitely use it many times, and it is great for making blankets and other garments. Don't avoid this one, try it and practice, you won't be sorry you did.

Not Learning How to Crochet in the Round

It is important to see how this works and then try it. This is vital to improving your crochet skills, so don't put off learning how to crochet in the round. It is a valuable technique to know how to use.

Not Learning How to Weave in Ends Properly

This is one of the most common mistakes made by beginners. It is so easy to just tie knots to the ends, but this is not the proper way of doing it and it is not neat either. Learn to weave the ends into the surface by using the tapestry needle to finish your work off.

Worrying About Your Mistakes

Making mistakes is what helps you learn and improve your work. Lots of practice and even more patience, as well as some creativity, is what makes a successful crocheted. You will have to undo your stitches from time to time, or even start over again, but that is fine. You are not only learning how to follow instructions; you are also getting used to using your tools and materials, so be patient.

Trying Out Complex Patterns First

So often, ladies are in a hurry to create the most beautiful colorful garments without being able to master the stitches or change their yarn colors. This could result in a disaster which could also be incredibly discouraging. Just keep it simple until you are confident with basic crochet work.

Giving Up Too Soon

It is too easy to just pick up your crochet hook, try out a few stitches, and then give up if they don't work. You might feel as though you are getting nowhere, but that is not true. Give yourself plenty of time to learn the basics because once you do that, then you can move forward and make so many items. If you cannot get your basic stitches right, then you will have problems making your item. Take it easy and things will slowly start coming together.

Even the most skillful people struggled at first. So go for it and enjoy it!

Chapter 8:
Simple Afghan Patterns

Basic Yo-Yo Pattern Afghan

A yo-yo afghan gives a unique circular pattern. It's fun and very different, so it will leave you with a product to be proud of! The pattern is worked in rounds.

Materials Needed:

- Hook: I-9
- Yarn: 1 skein of worsted weight yarn (approx. 62" of yarn needed).
- Tapestry needle.
- Gauge swatch: 24 stitches = 4 inches

Pattern Instructions:

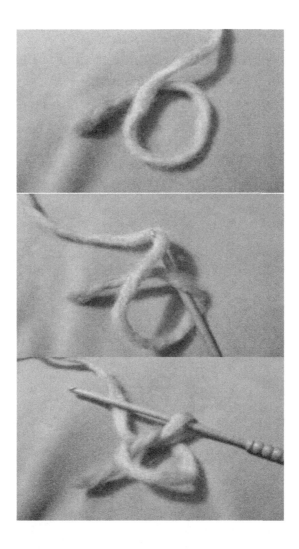

1. Create a slip knot and chain 4 stitches. Join these with a slip stitch in the first chain to create a ring.

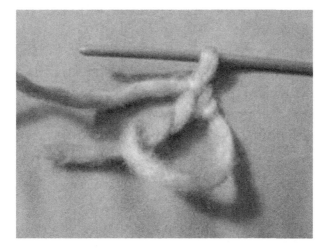

1. For the first round, Chain 3 as the first double crochet, work 11 more double crochet stitches in the ring, and fasten off.
2. Use the flat braid joins method for the first yo-yo

3. Join with a single crochet in any double crochet.
4. Chain 3, then single crochet in the next double crochet 11 times.
5. Join with a slip stitch in the first single crochet.
6. Fasten off.

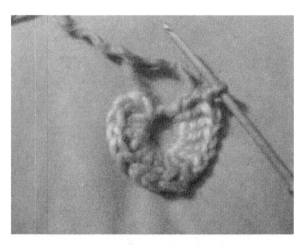

7. For the second yo-yo, join with a single crochet in one of the double crochet stitches.
8. Chain 3, then single crochet in the double crochet 9 times.
9. Chain 1.
10. Single crochet (inserting the hook from the bottom) in any chain-3 space on the first yo-yo.
11. Chain 1, then single crochet in the next double crochet on the second yo-yo.
12. Chain 1, then single crochet in the next chain-3 space on the first yo-yo.
13. Chain 1, then single crochet in the next double crochet on the second yo-yo.
14. Chain 3, then join with a slip stitch in the first single crochet on the second yo-yo.
15. Fasten off.

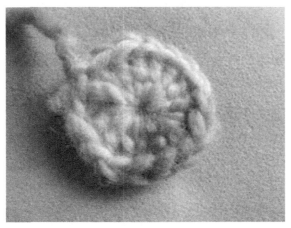

1. For the third yo-yo, join in loops 1 and 2 as done with the 2nd yo-yo

Checkerboard Stitch Afghan

The checkerboard stitch afghan is suitable for those cool summer evenings. It may not produce the warmest product, but it looks amazing.

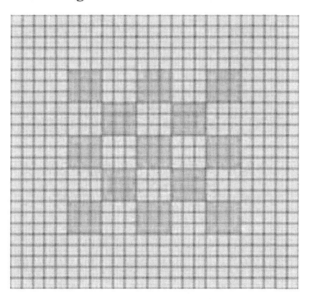

Materials Needed:

- Blanket size:46" by 63"
- Hook: F-5
- Yarn: 3 skeins of worsted weight yarn
- Other Materials: Tapestry needle
- Gauge Size: 15 stitches = 4 inches

Pattern Instructions:

1. Make a slip knot and chain 101 stitches. Double crochet in the 3rd stitch from the hook, then again in the next stitch.

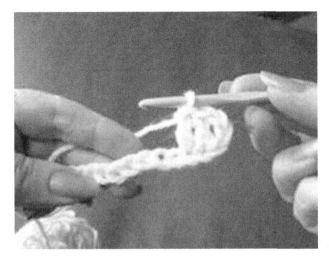

2. Chain 3, miss out on the next 3 stitches.

3. Double crochet in each of the next 3 stitches.

4. Repeat steps 2 and 3 across the row. Be sure to finish a double crochet in the last stitch.

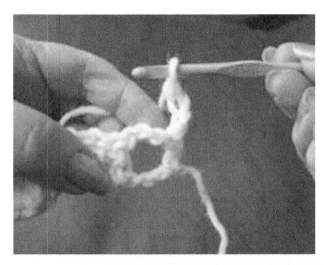

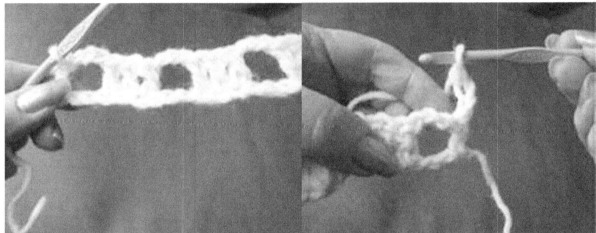

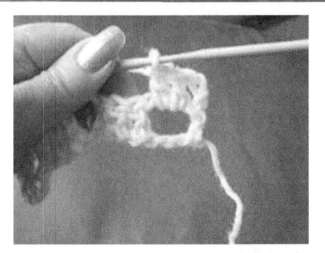

5.   Chain 3 and turn.

6.   Create 2 double crochet stitches in the chain-3 space of the former row. The chain 3 obtains the place of the first double crochet.

7.   Chain 3 stitches and 3 double crochet in the chain-3 space of the earlier row.

8. Repeat step 6 across the row.

9. Repeat all the above steps until the afghan is the desired length.
10. Finish off.

Easy Ripple Afghan

The ripple design looks great in a variety of colors and will look really impressive for a gift or in your own home.

Materials Needed:

- Blanket size: 40" by 60"
- Hook: I-9
- Yarn: Worsted weight yarn in a variety of colors
- Tapestry needle
- Scissors
- Gauge size: 4 stitches = 1 inch

Pattern Instructions:

1. Make a slip knot and chain 178 stitches.
2. For the first row, double crochet in the 3rd chain from the hook.
3. Double crochet in the next 6 chains.
4. Work 3 double crochet stitches in the next chain.
5. Double crochet in the next 6 chains.
6. Work a 3 stitch decrease in the next 3 chains.
7. Double crochet in the next 6 chains.
8. Work 3 double crochet stitches in the next chain.
9. Double crochet in the next 6 chains.
10. Repeat above 4 across the row.
11. Finish by working a 2-stitch decrease in the last 2 chains.
12. Chain 2 and turn.

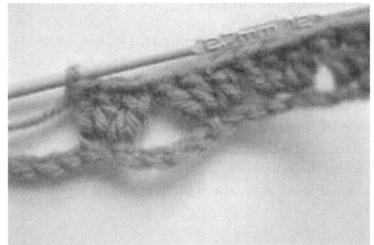

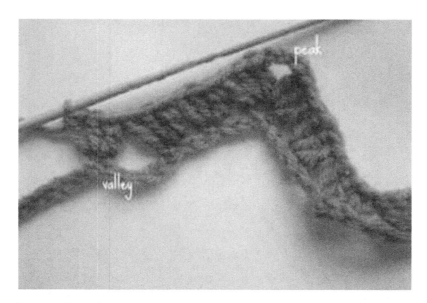

1. For the second row, skip the first stitch.
2. Double crochet in the next 7 stitches.
3. Work 3 double crochet stitches in the next double crochet.
4. Double crochet in the next double crochet stitches.
5. Work a 3-stitch decrease in the next 3 chains.
6. Double crochet in the next 6 chains.
7. Work 3 double crochet stitches in the next chain.
8. Double crochet in the next 6 chains.
9. Repeat above 4 across the row.
10. Finish by working a 2-stitch decrease in the last 2 chains.
11. Chain 2 and turn.

12. Repeat row 2 until the afghan is the desired length, changing colors as you like, then fasten off.

Chapter 8:
Some Crochet Patterns

Solomon's Knot Stitch

Solomon's knot is an openwork technique that is perfect for bathing suit cover-ups, long vests, or any other cloth that you want to wear. After several rows of Solomon's knot, the pattern begins to resemble the fishing pattern. The size of the stitch changes depending on how long or short the loop is drawn; some patterns use ¼ inch, ½ inch, or even as large as 3 inches! This is a fun stitch to add to your crochet technique repertoire—it can be added to a project for a bit of interest or flair or used to complete an entire project.

You can do Solomon's knot as small or as large as you wish. Once you get the hang of it, you can create a tighter, smaller weave that is great for fashion scarves or fingerless gloves, and it even looks great as decoration over plain patterns. Remember to keep your tension steady, this will help you create evenly spaced stitches that will look better when the project is complete.

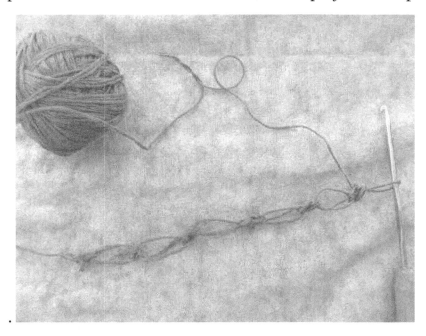

Pattern Instructions:

1. Ch 2 then sc in the first stitch.
2. Pull up the loop on your hook, enlarge it by tugging upward until you reach the height in the pattern; in this case, make it about 1 inch

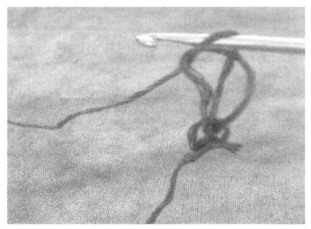

3. Yarn over and pull through the long loop on the hook. Pull up the yarn on the hook until it is as long as the yarn in the back.

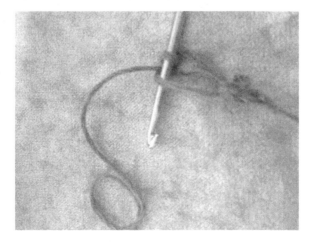

4. Put your hook under the yarn in the back and yo, then pull through the first loop on the hook.

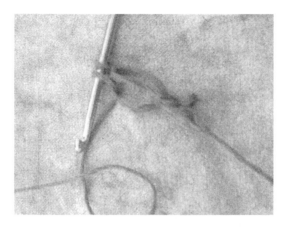

5. Yo and pull through both loops on the hook.
6. To crochet the next knot, pull up the last loop on your hook to make it an inch long and repeat steps 3 to 5.

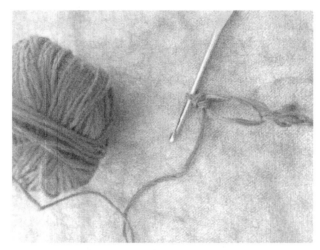

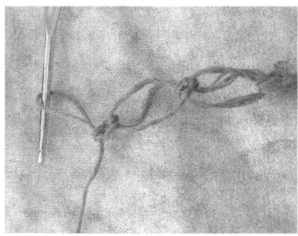

Here are a few items created using Solomon's knot stitch.

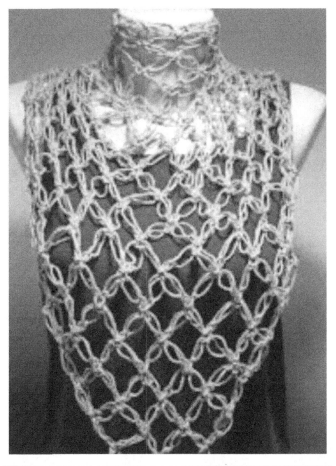

Waffles Stitch

The waffle stitch looks like the stitches in a thermal shirt, only on a much larger scale. This stitch is great for all types of warm items. The closeness of the waffle stitch and the bulk it creates is extra warm for blankets, scarves, and other items for keeping warm. The texture is a nice touch for throw pillows and roll pillows. Here are a few items created with the waffle stitch:

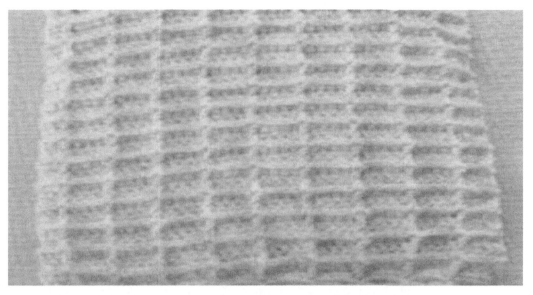

Pattern Instructions:

The waffle stitch is easy to do, just follow these instructions to create squares for your sampler.

1. Ch 30 then single crochet in each stitch across the row. Now ch 3, then dc in each stitch across the row. Now ch 3 and fpdc (same as bpdc only you insert the hook from the back to the front, the post will be in front of the hook) around the next post. Now dc in the next stitch. It should look like this:

2. Now you are going to alternate between the fpdc stitch and a dc stitch across the row. Keep track and make sure you are alternating or the pattern will not look right and you will have to start over.

3. Once the row is complete, ch 3, then dc in the next stitch, and fpdc in the next stitch. Again, you are going to alternate between dc and fpdc, the dc will end up in each fpdc from the last row, and the fpdc will end up in the dc from the previous row. Continue alternating until the row is complete.

4. Now ch 3, and repeat the pattern of dc and fpdc, making sure each dc is completed in an fpdc, and each fpdc is completed in a dc. Continue until the end of the row.

5. Continue repeating this row alternation and pattern until you have created a square similar in size to the others you have. Now you know how to do the waffle stitch! Crochet a few of these for your sampler, then move on to the next awesome stitch!

Here is a picture of a completed square done with the waffle stitch:

The waffle knit is textured and a bit bulky, but using a lighter-weight yarn such as sport yarn will make it softer and lighter for making scarves and shawls. This stitch is a close-knit and the tight stitches keep cold air from blowing through, it works great for blankets and lap blankets.

The texture is perfect for pillows too. Try making two of your squares of at least 20 square inches. Sew them inside out together with a large plastic yarn needle. Stuff it with some poly-fluff filling and you will have yourself a nice pillow.

You can even make covers for the pillow you already have, don't stuff it but fold in the side you are going to leave open. When you are finished, insert your pillow and pull the folded piece over the end to hide the opening!

The Bullion Stitch

The bullion stitch is a thick textured stitch that is perfect for blankets and scarves. To create the bullion stitch with ease, make sure you yo or wrap your yarn loosely around the hook. This makes it easier to pull the hook and yarn through the loops without getting caught up.

This stitch can be worked straight up and down in rows, or it can be worked across by skipping a few stitches between the beginning and end of the bullion stitch. This is also used in embroidery, and it can be used the same way on a finished crochet project to add interest by using yarn to embroider a design.

The stitch you are learning now is worked in every stitch across. This will give you a bullion that is straight up and down across the row. Remember to work loose but not too loose, you want to be able to pull the yarn through your wraps without getting it stuck or unraveling it.

Pattern Instructions:

1. This stitch is created by wrapping the yarn around, or multiple yo's. Ch 20 then ch 1 and turn, now yo 5 times or the number of times in your pattern.

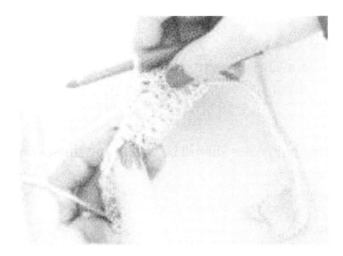

2. Put your hook into the next ch st and then, yo, and pull through all the loops on the hook.
3. Yo and sc 1 then yo 5 and put your hook into the next ch st and then yo and pull through all the loops on the hook, go slowly to avoid getting stuck.
4. Continue creating bullion stitches until you reach the end of the row, then ch 1 and repeat steps 1–3 until you reach the desired length.

Here are a few finished rows of crochet using the bullion stitch.

Little Angel

A wonderful decoration for a Christmas tree will be a little angel. How to make such an unusual decoration?

Materials Needed:

- Yarn (2 colors). The main color should be white, and the second may be gold, silver, or blue.
- A hook (1 mm diameter)
- Material to fill the toy.

Pattern Instructions:

1. Start knitting with the head of an angel. Take a white thread, then make a loop.

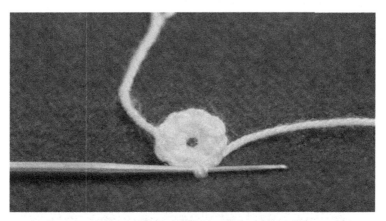

2. Tie the loop with the 8 single crochets.
3. In the second row knit each loop twice with a single crochet.
4. In the third row, knit the loop twice, but only every third loop.
5. Then knit 3 rows without changing the number of loops.

6. Now slowly begin to diminish the circle. Reduce every fourth loop.
7. At this stage fill the head with the chosen material.
8. Within the next two rows of knitting, you have to leave a circle with six loops.
9. Then knit 2 rounds without changing the number of loops.
10. Now we are getting to the dress.

11. In the first row, knit each loop twice with a double crochet.
12. In the second row, knit every first loop twice with a double crochet and miss every second loop.
13. In the third row, knit every second loop three times and miss every first loop.
14. In the fourth and fifth rows, simply repeat the pattern.

15. In the following 2 rows knit as follows - knit each loop four times with the double crochet. Your angel's dress is now ready.

16. Take a different color thread and tie it to the edge of the dress.

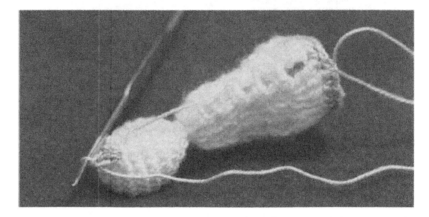

17. Now it's time to do the halo. Knit each loop three times over the head. Grab a loop near the neck and make 8 chains.

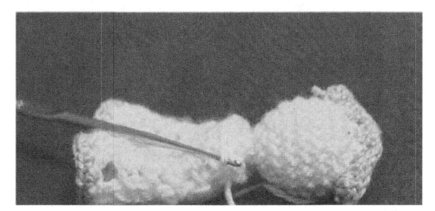

18. Connect the chain with the next loop in a circle. Finish the circle.

19. Now let's do the wings. Grab a loop and knit it with 6 double crochets. Next, take the middle loop and make 4 double crochets. Then make a chain and finish with 4 double crochets.
20. Do the same with the other wing.

A wonderful decoration Little Angel for a Christmas tree

21 Tie the wings around with another color. Done!

Little Fish for Children

Children are very fond of different toys with unusual textures. Besides, these products develop imagination and motor skills, which are essential for the first years of life. In the master class, a detailed scheme is shown below:

For this fish we need:

Materials Needed:

- Natural yarn (orange and white colors)
- Hook (1 millimeter diameter)
- Some wool yarn.

Pattern Instructions:

1. Start with making a loop with orange thread and tie it. Then knit 8 single crochets.

2. Bring up the knitting in the ordinary circle and pull it together hard enough.

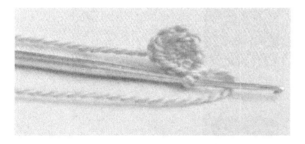

3. Next, knit according to the scheme.

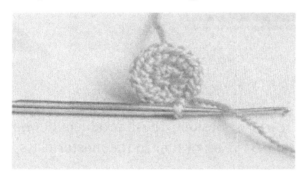

4. In the first row, knit each loop twice.
5. In the second row, row - knit similarly without changes.
6. In the third row, knit every second loop twice.
7. In the fourth row, knit without changes.
8. In the fifth row, change the thread for the white one. Do not change the number of loops.

9. In the sixth and seventh rows, go back to the orange thread and knit 2 rows with it.
10. In the eighth row, knit the first 3 loops with orange thread. You will need a white thread for the next 4 loops. Finish the remaining 3 loops with orange thread. Symmetrically knit the second half of the row.

11. In the ninth row, knit with the white thread.
12. In the tenth row, reduce every third loop.
13. At this stage, you need to fill the toy with some wool yarn.

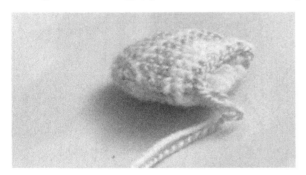

14. In the eleventh row, reduce every third loop.
15. In the twelfth row, reduce every third loop again.
16. In the thirteenth row, knit without changing the number of loops.
17. In the fourteenth row, switch the color to orange and knit without changing the number of loops.

11. And finally, we come to the tail. Pull the edge at one side and knit

12. Make 7 double treble crochets.

13. To knit the fin, catch a loop near the head and knit treble crochets along the back.

14. Then sew the eyes and the toy is ready!

Little fish for children

Crochet Potholder (Single Crochet)

Making a potholder and crocheting the pattern in this guide is an achievement to every beginner in the hobby of crocheting. What's good about this potholder guide is that you will be crocheting something that has practical use in the kitchen. In this guide, you will practice making the last and also the first stitch in one row of a single crochet. I hope you enjoy this guide!

Materials Needed:

- Balls of cotton (Varying colors depending on your preference)
- Crochet hook (size 9–5.5 mm is best)

Pattern Instructions:

1. Start with the ball of cotton with the color that you prefer to be inside. After this, chain 31.

2. In the first row, simply crochet into the chain, and in the second chain, start using single crochet until you reach the end of the row (which is 30 stitches).
3. In the second row, after just chain 1, turn your crochet the other way to start the second row. It may help you mark the number of stitches on a piece of paper so that you would not lose count while stitching.

4. Pick up two loops on top of those stitches, and then simply single crochet again (30 stitches). Once you reach the end, you have now finished the 2nd row. Keep track of the count to avoid any errors in the process.

5. From the third to the thirtieth, after the end of each row, simply chain 1, turn the crochet around and apply single crochet until the end of the row (30 stitches), keep count!

6. Repeat these instructions until you have finished the 30th row. It should look something like the picture below.

7. After finishing the 30th stitch, cut the end of the yarn (at least 4 inches of allowance) then pull it through the last loop at the end of the row. Make sure to pull it tight enough and secure it with a knot (binding off).

8. Repeat all the instructions at the top and create another one. Check the picture above. Use the other color that you picked, by the way. This side is the outer part of the potholder. But remember not to cut the end of the yarn on this second attempt.

9. In attaching these two pieces, you would need to create the other one having its rows sideward and the other one up and down. This is an IMPORTANT step in the whole guide. If you do not follow this correctly, you would not be able to create a potholder.

10. It should look something like the picture above. The back piece is the last one you have created and the one on top is the first one that you made. Make sure that your crochet hook is properly placed, as in the picture above.

11. On the back piece, chain 1 and do not turn the crochet around. Observe the picture below. After you have chained 1 you should put it through the two square layers. See the picture below.

12. The picture below shows how you should put it through the two layers.

13. Remember that your hook should be placed between the stitches in the first row for security. A more secure crochet results from this.

14. After crocheting the loose ends for 4–6 stitches, it is time to pull it a little to secure the whole row. Make sure not to pull it too tightly, though.

15. Slowly crochet along the edges of the squares. Be precise in stitching one layer to another row. Slowly bring the two squares together. You can also count the number of stitches from time to time and compare them to the rows. Make sure that you have not missed a single stitch in the process.

16. When you get to the corner, single crochet 3 times to create stitches on the same corner. This would allow you to properly place your crochet hook and allow it to move to the next side. Keep going on the other side and pick up row by row and stitch by stitch until the end. Repeat the process.

17. The picture shows loose ends (2, in fact). Simply go around both by single crocheting around 4–6 stitches. Pull the short end to make the whole structure secure. Don't forget to push the end between the two square layers. Keep going until the last loose end and repeat the process of single crocheting 4–6 stitches and pulling to secure.

18. Now on the third side, repeat the process of single crochet 3 around the corner and continue to the last side.
19. Single crochet then chains 6 more stitches and skip 2 stitches which would then lead to you slip stitching into the third one.
20. Now it's time to cut the yarn. Make sure to leave an allowance of at least 3 inches and pull it through the ending loop. Pull it and make a knot, making sure that it's secured well.

21. Hiding the thread that remains is easy. Simply put your crochet hook at the top and pull it inside to hide it. Make sure that it ends up inside the two square layers.

Congratulations! You have now created your own crochet potholder. You can use this to hold your pot and other hot utensils used for cooking since it has a very heat-resistant property that would prevent you from burning.

Baby Bib

A baby bib can save your baby's clothes from stains and also help you reduce the laundry. It's not a secret that kids love to play with food, so it is important to minimize the probability of getting it on the baby's clothing. There are a lot of bibs for babies in stores, and you can buy whichever you like or create your own baby bib in this crochet pattern guide.

What you need:

Materials Needed:

- Different colors of yarn
- Crochet hook no.2

81

Pattern Instructions:

1. Begin with making a chain of 30 loops. Knitting will be made in both directions with single crochets.
2. In the next 9 rows add one loop on both sides.
3. Change the color white to gray and knit three rows with single crochets.
4. Change the color to white again and knit number 22 rows with single crochets.
5. Further, we skip one loop on one side and make 11 rows with this pattern. We turn around the knitting, skip one loop and knit till the end with the single crochet.

6. Then we decrease the number of the loop only from the right side and skip in each second row one last loop.
7. The same work is done on the other side. Decrease the loops from the left side.
8. Tie around the bib with yarn.

And we get such a beautiful bib for a little boy. To make the same bib for a girl, just change the yarn colors to pink and red.

A Crochet Baby Bib

Chapter 9:
The Economic Part of Crocheting

Many people around the world have been able to learn crocheting skills. It is an industry that has grown and has empowered very many men and women around the world. This has greatly improved the economy. Below are some of the economic impacts of crocheting. Do crochets have an economic impact? Several people may not find crocheting beneficial. They may not see it as a source of income, but it contributes immensely to the economy.

During cold seasons, people look for things to keep them warm. They, therefore, have to purchase scarves, sweaters, socks, and other products made from yarn. This increases the rate of yarn production as a result of the increase in demand for crocheted items. This is said to lead to the growth of the economy. Below are some of the economic impacts brought by crocheting.

So many crocheting companies have been opened, which has created employment opportunities for many families around the world. They can take care of their families from the income they earn from the crocheting companies.

Women can crochet items and sell them to people in their neighborhood, which enables them to earn some money. This helps to improve the economy since they do not become dependent on the government for their survival. The government is, therefore, able to concentrate on other development projects since its people are not overly dependent on them. This acts as a source of income for certain people, which also helps in the growth of the economy.

The experts in this area have also taken up the role of training more people in crocheting. This ensures the empowerment of more people, which means more skilled individuals in a country.

Individuals who have specialized in information technology also develop apps that contain crochet instructions. This has helped people to have easy access to the skills, and anyone can install the app and learn the skills in their own free time.

Social and Traditional Impact of Crocheting

Crocheting has had a great impact on our society. The skill keeps on being passed on from one generation to another. This has helped a lot in impacting people's lives socially and even traditionally. Below are some social and traditional impacts brought about by crocheting?

For charity most often, we find ourselves with different types of crotchets, which we mostly make during our free time. One can craft some items and give them out to charities. It will always feel great when one benefits from an item crocheted with a lot of love. It will act as a way of showing your generosity and sense of care for others. One will feel good when someone appreciates something that was made purposely to suit one's needs.

Aesthetic Value

Crocheting can display the beauty of a tradition. Before the invention of big companies that dealt with the manufacturing of clothes, people used to wear crocheted clothes. Some people make crochets to beautify the environment. One, therefore, makes items that will make their environment calm. This will enable them to feel relaxed whenever they are around.

Crocheting BoostsSelf-Esteem

We all feel good when complimented for doing something so well. Compliments motivate us to produce crochets better than previous ones. When we sell the crafts we made or give them as a gift, it boosts our self-esteem. We feel great about our accomplishments. Self-esteem can also be built through learning new skills. One can feel productive, creating beauty through self-expression.

Crocheting Reduces Stress and Anxiety

We all get stressed up at some point in our life. We may become anxious as a result of the strenuous activities we may have engaged in our daily activities. One needs to give oneself a break. Getting a yarn and crocheting with it would be of great help in relaxing their mind. It is through the repetition of the stitches, as you count the rows, that your mind gets some kind of relaxation. All the anxiety thoughts are relieved since your focus is on creatively making the crochets.

It Eases and Relieves Depression

Our emotions keep changing depending on the occasion. For instance, in the grieving period, it seems impossible to overcome your grief. Most times we feel like the world has come to an end. Crocheting can be comforting during the grieving period. Crafting such as crocheting is said to be helpful in the stimulation of dopamine, which enables one to feel happier and emotionally stable.

It Keeps One Busy

Imagine you are left at home alone. No other work for you, you can choose to do some crocheting. You will be relaxing at the same time, keeping yourself busy. You don't have to create wonderful products out of it. The whole idea is to keep your mind engaged through a useful course that helps you earn some money or even contribute to charity. In a scenario where you are following up on a program on the television, your hands will be busy crafting while your eyes are glued to the television. The best thing about crocheting is that one can engage every member of the family. They will be able to contribute various ideas about what you are making, suggestions on colors, and even designs.

It Brings Communities Together

There are many ways to bring people together. One of them is having yarn crafting introduced to a community. They can have a meet-up in public to do crocheting. The organizers can organize a crochet fair along with related events. This will be of great help since people from different places will be able to meet and share ideas. They will be able to learn from one another, hence more creative designs. The community can even come together and build yarn stores which will benefit the community from the sales made in the store. All the participants can also buy the yarn at a reduced price which will enable them to make more crocheted items for sale. They will, in turn, become more productive, which brings economic empowerment amongst them.

Chapter 10: FAQs

Here is a quick roundup of the most common questions that are asked about how to best care for your yarn or wool.

Can You Wash an Entire Skein?

In some cases, you may need to wash the skeins or yarn balls before use (spillages, etc.) and although this can be difficult, it is possible. The trickiest part about this is to ensure that the yarn doesn't unravel, which you can do by putting it in a pair of tights or washing bag beforehand. However, make sure to follow the same washing guidelines and check to see that all detergent has been rinsed out (you may need to hand-rinse them to make sure as this could irritate if there is residue).

How Often Should You Wash Yarn or Wool?

This depends on the amount of wear and the purpose of the project. For example, a crochet bag may only need to be sponged down once in a while, whereas clothes would need to be washed more frequently. Clothes such as socks would definitely need to be washed after each use to avoid any fungal or bacterial infections, while a jumper may be worn a few times before needing to be washed. It entirely depends.

Can You Dye Your Own Yarn?

The answer to this is yes, and the easiest types of yarn to dye are animal fibers, for example, alpaca, wool, or mohair. Make sure to protect your skin and clothes when dying your own yarn as it easily transfers and can cause a large mess. For synthetic yarn, you will need to buy a specific dye to use for the fiber.

How Do You Find Yarn Care Instructions for Other Yarn?

Usually, yarn will come with a wraparound label that has specific washing instructions. Some special types of yarn will come with packet instructions, and others may not come with anything at all. The more specialized the yarn is, the more likely you are to get instructions. Generally speaking, worsted weight yarn, which is most commonly used, is also more durable, which means you are less likely to get specific instructions.

Can You Get Rid of Old Stains and Smells?

Yes, however, not always, and a lot of dried stains or lingering smells are hard to get rid of. The longer the stain or smell has been present on the fiber, the harder it is to get rid of.

Can You Tumble Dry?

It is best not to tumble dry yarn or wool as it is very sensitive to temperature and it can make it rough or coarse on the skin—as well as the risk of shrinking—if it is exposed to higher temperatures. If you choose to use the tumble dryer, it is best to do so on a cool or very low heat setting for short amounts at a time to check if it is not having adverse effects on the fibers.

How Long Can You Keep Yarn or Wool for?

Wool or yarn can be kept for a very long time—even years if it is stored properly in the right conditions and maintained. Wool that has been kept for over 10 years may not be viable for crocheting or knitting because it has started to degrade but this depends on the type. Organic fibers that haven't been treated may not last as long as store-bought that have been chemically treated.

How Do You Store Yarn?

Store in skeins or balls in a dry place and make sure to clean out and check frequently to avoid your stash coming into contact with a lot of dust, moths, or pests that might contaminate the supply. Besides, avoid getting your stash wet and ensure that you frequently air it out to avoid there being a musty smell embedded in the yarn.

How to Read Crochet Patterns?

To my opinion, reading a pattern of crochet is important for learning simple crochet. You are very limited when it comes to finished projects unless you can read crochet patterns!

If you can't read a pattern for a crochet, I think you are very tight. What are you doing, keep going until you think it is right and start like that?

You have the world at your fingertips if you can read a crochet pattern. You're not afraid to try new stuff in my opinion!

However, I am fascinated by the number of people who cannot understand crochet patterns. It seems like a real shame that they don't know how to get better and feel better about their efforts!

If you cannot read a pattern of crochet, how do you make home-made dishcloths or crochets? Remember, in the picture they look fast, but can you double that?

When I started to crochet (it seems to have been a lifetime), these patterns with such unusual abbreviations were a challenge for me. At this point, I decided to learn how to read the patterns, regardless.

I have done a lot of work, answered a variety of questions, and have eventually obtained results. The odd thing was that even I wasn't even crocheting wool alone.

To be able to read crochet patterns would seem to encourage you to go higher—that's how I switched to cotton and made doilies in a very short time, learning how to read patterns from crochet.

What scares me is that people who can't read crochet patterns don't seem to be careful to clarify and/or illustrate any of the crochet stitches on a one-on-one basis. This disturbs me.

I was told that it demonstrated a lack of maturity in someone who did crochet at home without being able to read crochet patterns. It did not have any ambition!

Now I'm not in agreement, but I've got one I can tell, "Don't learn half of anything, learn the whole thing, or waste your time!" I could crochet a doily while my oldest daughter was in the hospital at the age of five months, by reading crochet instructions.

Another Thing to Consider

How do you increase your own crocheting skills to include extra stitches if you can't read crochet instructions or patterns? I mean the triple stitch, the half-double stitch, and so on—it could be overwhelming!

And if you're a home crocheter, learn how to read the patterns that I call never-ending; extend your scope beyond your standards.

Conclusion

A lifetime talent where you'll use to make complete presents for others and pieces for your home and wardrobe is the delicate art of crocheting. Consider learning a few basic stitches, with more advanced basic stitches, expand on that. Next, find out what hook is most convenient for you in scale and design. Then, begin with basic yarns and patterns for beginners, and in no time, you will be a pro.

You don't need a lot of supplies to start crocheting. The crochet hook is the main item, and there are lots of various sizes and kinds. Choose one made of aluminum when you pick a beginner crochet needle, since the thread can help the yarn glide effortlessly. The three simple crochet supplies you're going to have included an I-9 or H-8 size aluminum crochet ring, whatever fits better in your hand, a wool or acrylic yarn skein or string, and scissors.

Start by gripping your crochet hook as you would hold a pencil, gripping the hook between your thumb and index finger at the tiny indentation in the center known as a finger hold. For ease and power, you should slip your third finger upwards towards the tip of the hook. The hook is going to be partially angled toward you but should not be facing downwards or upwards.

As one of the first things you need to remember to get acquainted with crocheting is putting a slip knot on the crochet hook. Turn and thread the yarn onto the hook easily, wrap the yarn under the hook and draw it to tighten around the loop. If it's uncomfortable at first; don't fear; just start training, and it'll get simpler.

Beginning crocheters typically start first by studying the row stitch. The chain stitch is one of the most important simple stitches that you would need to know since most crochet projects are focused on them. In a pattern, the chain stitch abbreviation for the plural form is "ch," or occasionally "chs." Usually, you can see "ch" following by a figure. Ch 135 means, for instance, that you can crochet 135 chain stitches.

Now that you know how to create a slip knot and simple stitches, you can take on a project for beginners. You may start with a baby blanket or even a scarf made for new crocheters. Without abbreviations for simplistic analysis, such beginner patterns can be useful—taking it gently when you begin your first project and be careful with yourself. It's all right if you have to start again at the start of the pattern.

Made in the USA
Las Vegas, NV
31 January 2024

85132170R00050